Ukulele Magic

BOOK 1

by Ian Lawrence

MMA
Medway Music Association

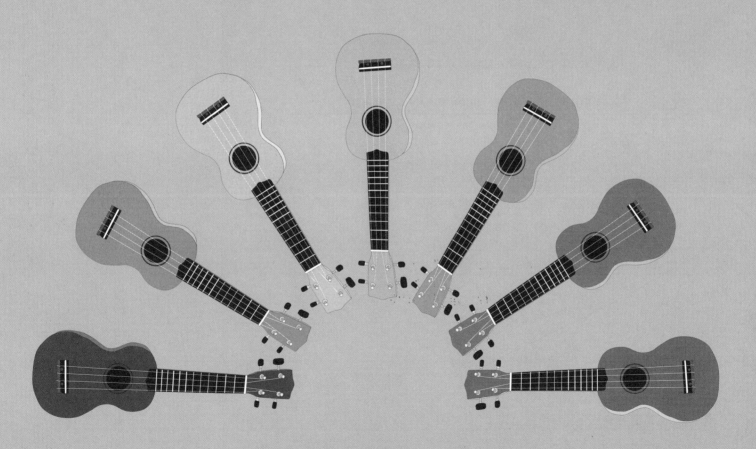

A&C BLACK · LONDON

Meet my ukulele

My ukulele has a body,
　　a neck and a head,

But it's got no arms and legs!

My ukulele has a body,
　　a neck and a head,

But it's got no arms and legs!

It has a bridge and a sound hole,
　　a fretboard and a nut,

Four strings and tuning pegs,

My ukulele has a body,
　　a neck and a head

But it's got no arms and legs!

head

neck

body

tuning

pegs

nut

fretboard

sound hole

bridge

Video　Audio 1　Audio 2

Learning objectives

★ To learn the parts of the ukulele.

Extras

Compare the parts of a ukulele with the parts of a guitar or a violin. Are they exactly the same?

That thumb brush strum

There once was a man in Tennessee (click the rhythm)

Kept cookies in his ukulele,

Now cookies are such crumbly things

He dropped some crumbs all over the strings.

Brushing the strings with his thumb

STRUM STRUM STRUM   STRUM STRUM

He discovered that thumb brush strum.

STRUM STRUM STRUM   STRUM STRUM

Brushing the strings, everyone!

STRUM STRUM STRUM   STRUM STRUM

Now we're playing that thumb brush strum!

STRUM STRUM STRUM   STRUM STRUM

FINGERTIPS

● Support the neck or
he head with your left
and without touching
he strings or the tuning
egs, while you play the
humb brush strum ▼
ith your right hand
humb.

● Use the side of your
ight hand thumb to
rush the strings (just as
you were sweeping
way those cookie
rumbs).

● Keep your sleeve out
f the way!

Video Audio 3 Audio 4

Learning objectives

★ To learn • the correct playing position •
the thumb brush strum.

★ To sing and play alternately with accuracy.

Extras

This song is based on one by Bo
Diddley, and features his trademark
rhythmic strumming pattern.

Unit 1

Meet my ukulele

G C E A

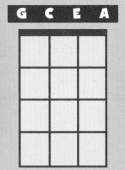

FINGERTIPS

● **Four strings we play**
The thumb rest stroke ▼ is like a slow motion thumb brush ~ the thumb comes to rest on the next string.

● Play each string with a rest stroke. Keep playing G C E A as you sing.

● **Checking the pitch**
Sing the song. Players 1 and 2, standing back to back, each play an open string rest stroke. Did Player 2's note sound higher or lower?

PLAY REST STROKES

▼   ▼   ▼   ▼
G   **C**   **E**   **A**

SING

**G C E A,
Four strings we play,
When we tune our ukuleles
Every day.**

Checking the pitch

ALL SING

**Higher or lower or staying the same
Checking the pitch is a listening game.**

PLAYER 1
▼

PLAYER 2
▼

G C E A

Learning objectives

★ To learn • the open string names • the thumb rest stroke • a repeated pattern.

★ To identifying higher and lower pitch.

Extras

A repeating pattern might be called a 'riff' or a 'loop' or an 'ostinato'. Listen to the riff in **Summer Nights** (Grease).

Video   **Video**   **Audio 5**   **Audio 6**   **Audio 7**   **Audio 8**

Stringalong rag

Meet my ukulele

G C E A

PLAY

▼ ▼ ▼ ▼

G	G	G	G
C	C	C	C
E	E	E	E
A	A	A	A
G	G	G	G
C	C	C	C
E	E	A	A
G	G	C	C

FINGERTIPS

● This piece has a slow, steady pulse. Try tapping the pulse before you attempt to play the rest strokes.

● Join in after the introduction, listening carefully to the track as you play. Relax and try not to rush.

    Video Audio 9

Learning objectives

★ To play open string rest notes to accompany a recorded piece of music, keeping a steady pulse.

Extras

This is in the style of a piano rag by the African-American composer Scott Joplin. Ragtime music was an early form of jazz at the beginning of the 20th century.

It's raining, it's pouring

SING x3

It's raining, it's pouring,

The old man is snoring,

He went to bed and he bumped his head

And he couldn't get up in the morning.

RAP

Get up, get up, get up, get out of bed!

It doesn't matter what the weatherman said.

You may be getting old, you may have bumped your head

But you've gotta get to work to keep the family fed!

SING X 1

It's raining, it's pouring,

The old man is snoring,

He went to bed and he bumped his head

And he couldn't get up in the morning.

FINGERTIPS

● Practise singing and rapping this before you add the Rainy Patterns.

● In the rap section the words are not sung but spoken so concentrate on making the word rhythms really accurate and 'punchy'.

Video   **Audio 10**   **Audio 11**

Learning objectives

★ To perform a song with two very contrasted styles.

Extras

Rappers often borrow an existing song like this one and add their own spin to it. Think of some examples or adapt another well-known song.

Unit 2

Opening it up

G C E A

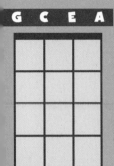

song   rap

SING

It's rain-ing, it's pour-ing...

RAP

Get up, get up, get...

UKULELE 1

E   C

Drip   drop

UKULELES 1-2

C   C

UKULELE 2

Splash

BEAT BOX

Boo-boom   cha

UKULELE 3 · FREE STROKES

G   A   G   A

Pit - ter   pat - ter

FINGERTIPS

● Add these rainy patterns to **It's Raining, It's Pouring** one at a time or divide into three groups of players so you can play them all together the last time through.

● Ukulele 3 plays a banjo finger style with free strokes of the thumb ↗ and first finger ↖. They are 'free' because they don't 'rest' on the next string.

● Add xylophones playing in the rap section.

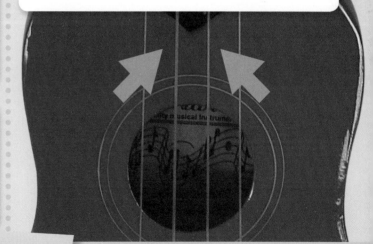

Learning objectives

★ To learn • the free stroke • different types of accompaniment ★ To perform them at the same time in a group performance.

Extras

Listen to **April Showers** (Bambi) · **Jardins Sous La Pluie** by Debussy · **Pula ea na (It's Raining)** by the South African trumpeter Hugh Masakela.

   Video Audio 10 Audio 11

Ukulele strummer

FINGERTIPS

● Make up a new strumming rhythm in the gap after the song. Use your right hand first finger to play:
- down strokes ↓
- up strokes ↑
- shuffle strums (down up strokes) ↓↑

● You can use the thumb brush strum to play your rhythms but faster patterns are easier with first finger strokes and shuffles.

SING

Ukulele **strummer**,
Can you **play** us something **new?**
If you strum a **rhythm,**
Maybe we can copy **you!**
One two three four
Off you go!

LEADER

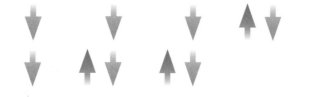

ALL COPY

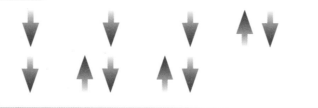

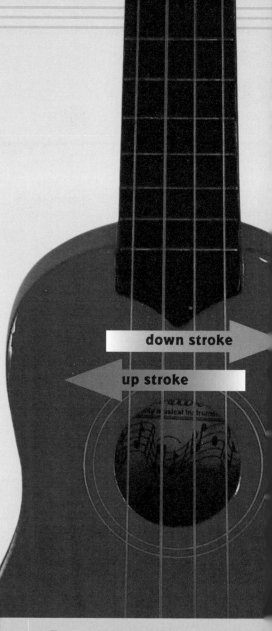

down stroke

up stroke

Video   **Audio 12**   **Audio 13**

Learning objectives

★ To learn • first finger down stroke • first finger up stroke • shuffle strum (down up).

★ Improvise and echo rhythms.

Extras

With some friends, choose four songs that you all know. Take turns to sing one of them in your head and strum the rhythm of the words. Can the others identify it?

Opening it up

Starlight star bright

G C E A

FINGERTIPS

● To play the banjo finger style, play free strokes with thumb and first finger.

● Make up some more starry accompaniment sounds to give a shimmering starlight effect. Metal percussion (triangles, bell trees, etc) work well. You could also play the banjo pattern on three chime bars, a glockenspiel or a metallophone.

UKULELE 1 · BANJO STYLE FREE STROKES

G   A   G   E   G   A   G   E

UKULELE 2 · THUMB BRUSH STRUM

Star - light   star   bright   first   star   I   see tonight...

SING

Starlight star bright, first star I see tonight,
Wish I may wish I might, have the wish I wish tonight.

    Video Audio 14 Audio 15

Learning objectives

★ To play an arrangement with a banjo finger style or strummed open strings.

★ To create a calm, peaceful mood.

Extras

Check out the final few minutes of **The Planets Suite** by Gustav Holst and listen to the sounds he chose to create a starry effect.

FINGERTIPS

● Hold up your left hand 'high five' style and tap the tip of each finger as you sing the song.

● Mix up the numbers and display them on a card to try new combinations of fingers.

1 is for pointing

2 is tall,

3 can wear a wedding ring and

4 is small.

For ukulele the finger numbers go:

1 2 3 4

So now you know!

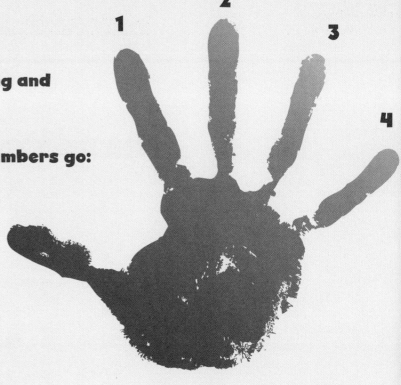

Try: 4 3 2 1 or 1 3 2 4

Video   Audio 16   Audio 17

Learning objectives

★ To learn ● the left hand finger numbers for ukulele playing.

Extras

Pianists also number their fingers but they include their thumbs:

1 2 3 4 5

Our first chord

C MAJOR

[chord diagram showing 3rd fret]
3

1 2
3
4

FINGERTIPS

• Keep your left hand thumb on the back of your ukulele's neck and your third finger up on its tip ~ this lets you pinch down on the A string without touching the others accidentally.

• When we hold down the A string at the third fret the note changes from A to C. This means that the instrument is now sounding only the notes of the C major chord C, E and G

C MAJOR

[strum arrows]

Frere Jacques, Frere Jacques,

Dormez vous? Dormez vous?

Sonnez les matines! Sonnez les matines!

Ding, dang, dong! Ding, dang, dong!

C MAJOR

3 third fret

   Video **Audio 18** **Audio 19**

Learning objectives
★ To learn • how to play the chord of C major • to use it to accompany a familiar song.

Extras
Play a C major strum with: Kookaburra sits in the old gum tree; Row row row your boat.

Unit 3

Our first chord

C MAJOR

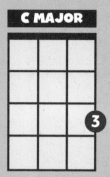

verse

chorus

UKULELE 1

C   A   G   A   C   A   G   A

SING

Three little children lying in bed,
Two were sick and the other almost dead,
Sent for the doctor, the doctor said,
'Feed those children on shortnin' bread.'

UKULELE 2

C MAJOR

SING

Mammy's little baby loves shortnin'   shortnin',
Mammy's little baby loves shortnin'   bread.

FINGER TIPS

- Remember to play banjo style with thumb and first finger free strokes.

- Some people find the banjo finger-picking style easier than others. Don't worry if you find it tricky: just join in strumming the C chord.

- For the strummed section, try out the thumb brush or down stroke.

page 12

Video   Audio 20   Audio 21

Learning objectives

★ To learn • to play an American banjo style pattern • to keep a steady pulse throughout.

Extras

Check out some American bluegrass countr music for some good examples of the amazingly complex and rhythmical banjo finger-style patterns.

Our first chord

C MAJOR

3

FINGERTIPS

- Sing the verse and follow the strumming directions, then improvise your own strumming fills on the words 'strum chord C'.

- Use down and up strokes, shuffle strums and thumb brush strums.

SING AND STRUM

C

Strum three down strokes ~   one two three

Strum three up strokes ~   one two three

Strum three down strokes ~   one two three

?

Find another way to strum chord C.

It's up to you, not down to me,

?

Find another way to strum chord C. (repeat)

Video   Audio 22   Audio 23

Learning objectives

★ To make up new strumming patterns, responding to the rhythms of the music.

Extras

Try these patterns:

A minor miracle

A minor miracle

A minor

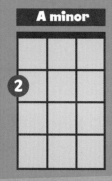

FINGERTIPS

● When playing the A minor chord your left hand second finger has to reach right across the fretboard to hold down the fourth string. To avoid accidentally touching any of the other strings make sure your thumb is behind the neck and your finger is curved over and that you are placing your fingertip on the string.

● When you see the hand symbol, damp the strings by placing the heel of your right hand quickly over them to stop the sound.

STRUM

A minor

     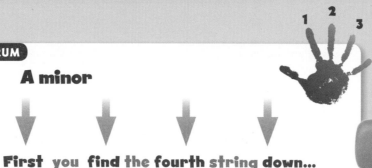

First you find the fourth string down...

SING AND STRUM

First you find your fourth string
down on fret number two,
Put your second finger there
it's easy to do.
There's A minor miracle just
waiting for you.

A minor

STRUM   STRUM   STRUM   DAMP!

U - ku - le - le Ma - gic!

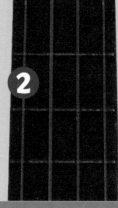

A minor

second fret ②

page 14

    Video Audio 24 Audio 25

Learning objectives

★ To learn • to play the A minor chord • how to damp the strings.

Extras

Strum the A minor chord to **Canoe Song** (My paddle's keen and bright). Can you use the string damp technique in your accompaniment?

Unit 4

A minor miracle

Autumn leaves

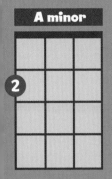

A minor

UKULELE 1 • TREMOLO STRUM

A minor

UKULELE 2

A minor

Autumn leaves are falling...

SING

Autumn leaves are falling
Red and gold and brown,
Twisting, turning
Floating to the ground.

FINGERTIPS

● You can create a magical effect, like the autumn wind rustling the leaves on the trees, by using a tremolo strum. Finger an A minor chord and rub your RH first finger lightly and quickly, up and down across the strings half way along the fretboard.

● This is a gentle song. Use a thumb brush strum half way along the fretboard to give a soft, sweet sound.

A minor

2

Video

Audio 26

Audio 27

Learning objectives

★ To learn • to play the tremolo strum • to play a gentler thumb brush strum.

Extras

Use the tremolo strum and the A minor chord to play **Shalom Chaverim.**

Unit 4
Autumn leaves in TAB
A minor miracle

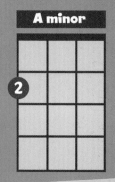

A minor

2

FINGER**TIPS**

● TAB (tablature) is used for instruments like guitars and ukuleles. It tells you which notes to play. The four lines represent the four strings of your ukulele. A zero on the line means play the open string; 3 means press the string at the third fret.

● Play each note with RH thumb rest strokes.

● Play each accompaniment part in turn as you repeat the song, or divide into four ukulele groups to play them all together.

UKULELES 1 AND 2

A minor

Autumn leaves are falling,

Red and gold and brown,

Twisting, turning

Floating to the ground.

UKULELE 3

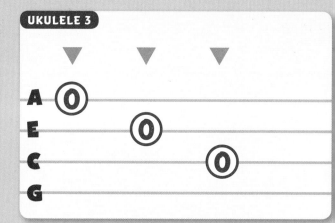

UKULELE 4

    Video Audio 26 Audio 27

Learning objectives

★ To develop an accompaniment for a song about autumn leaves, using patterns that fall in pitch.

Extras

Invent tuned percussion patterns that fall in pitch to accompany the song. Take all the bars off a tuned percussion instrument except A E C and low A. Make up your falling patterns on these.

minor miracle

A minor

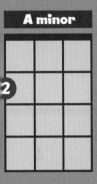

2

FINGERTIPS

● This Canadian Inuit canoe song not only helped to pass the time on a journey but also helped keep the paddles in time.

● Say the words 'Hi hiya Hi hiya' to help with the 'down down up, down down up' strumming rhythm.

● Compose a quiet, floating introduction using the tremolo again and some glittering, watery sounds on percussion.

STRUM

A minor

Hi   hi - ya Hi   hi - ya

SING

Land of the silver birch,

Home of the beaver.

Where still the mighty moose

Wanders at will.

Blue lake and rocky shore,

I will return once more

Hi hi ya Hi hi ya

Hi hi ya Hi hi ya

Hi hi ya

HI!

Video   Audio 28   Audio 29

Learning objectives

★ To learn to play a repeated strumming rhythm to accompany a song.

Extras

Much of the music of First Nation North Americans was sung with a simple rhythmical drum accompaniment. Add some drums, softly beating the strumming pattern.

F major march

F MAJOR

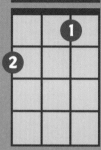

CHORUS · SING AND STRUM

F MAJOR

We're playing F   strum strum
Oh yes!   strum strum   (x2)

1ST VERSE · SING

Finger number **1** and finger number **2**
Using them together, **see** what you can **do**.

CHORUS · SING AND STRUM

2ND VERSE · SING

First fret on the **E** string, second on the **G**,
Using them together, **strum** along with **me**.

CHORUS · SING AND STRUM

CODA

Left right **left** right **left** right **left**
we're playing **F!**

FINGERTIPS

● This song is in a march style so try to sing and play it with a very disciplined military rhythm.

● First practise finding the F major chord with fingers 1 and 2.

● Play thumb brush or down stroke strums.

F MAJOR

first fret   1

second fret   2

    Video Audio 30   Audio 31

Learning objectives
★ To learn • to identify the correct fingers and frets to play an F major chord • to use the chord in a marching song.

Extras
Listen to **March** from **The Love of Three Oranges** by Sergei Prokofiev • **The Liberty Bell March** by the American John Philip Sousa who wrote so many he was known as the March King.

Baboushka

FIRST SEQUENCE X 2

Am   Am   F   Am

Rid-ing thro' the win-ter snow...

SECOND SEQUENCE X 2

Am   F   Am

Sleigh bells jingling as she goes...

minor   **F MAJOR**

FINGERTIPS

● Play an F major chord. Lift finger 1 off the E string to make the A minor chord shape.

● Practise lifting finger 1 off the E string and placing it back again to change chord.

● Play each sequence twice, repeating this pattern throughout the song:

Am Am F Am   echo
Am F Am    echo

● The verse and chorus combine last time round.

UKULELE 1   **UKULELE 2**

verse

Riding through the winter snow,   echo

Sleigh bells jingling as she goes,   echo

Christmas Eve, Baboushka comes   echo

With a present for everyone.   echo

chorus

All over Russia   echo

They listen for the sleigh,   echo

Christmas is coming   echo

Baboushka's on her way.   echo

first fret — **1**

second fret — **2**

   Video **Audio 32** **Audio 33**

Learning objectives

★ To perform an echo song (call and response) using two chords.

Extras

Build up a wintry atmosphere by adding sleigh bells. ● Other songs that work with these two chords include **Beat Again** by JLS and **Eleanor Rigby** by Lennon and McCartney

C7   **F MAJOR**

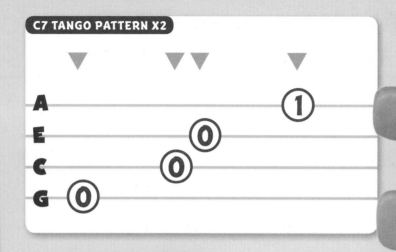

C7 TANGO PATTERN X2

A — ① (at far right)
E — ⓪
C — ⓪
G — ⓪

F MAJOR TANGO PATTERN X2

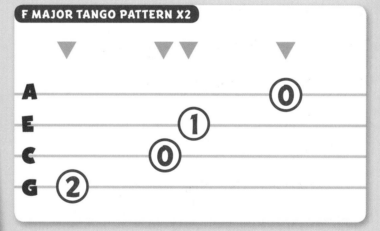

A — ⓪
E — ①
C — ⓪
G — ②

FINGERTIPS

● Find the F major chord shape with fingers 1 and 2. Practise moving finger number 1 to the new C7 chord shape and back to F.

● Listen to TAB Tango and practise the F major and C7 patterns using rest strokes. Take your time ~ do it slowly at first. When each pattern is secure, try changing from one to the other and back again: **C7 C7 F F**...

● Tango music must be played with a strong, accurate rhythm. Tap out the rhythm as you listen to the track before you play along with it.

   Video **Audio 34**

Learning objectives
★ To learn to play a repeated tango pattern made from two chords and written in TAB.

Extras
Tango is a dramatic dance that came from Argentina. Tango music has very distinctive Latin rhythm patterns.

Calypso strum

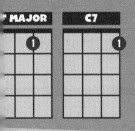

F MAJOR   C7

CALYPSO STRUM

Down down-up   up-down

FINGERTIPS

● Practise the calypso strum on open strings until it feels confident. Play it with first finger down and up strokes.

● When playing the down stroke you need to have your finger nail brushing the strings, so make sure your finger points towards the floor and not towards the head of the ukulele.

● When you're confident with the strum, practise the turnaround chord sequence: **F C7 C7 F** x2

● Play along with the audio. Can you sing at the same time?

● When you play the xylophone part say the words to help you with the rhythm.

SING AND CALYPSO STRUM

F   **C7**
Down down-up up-down, down in Kingston town

C7   **F**
When the Carnival comes,

        F   **C7**
They sing calypso, and play calypso

         C7   **F**
With down down-up up-down strums.

XYLOPHONE

A	A	A	C		C	A		Bb	Bb	Bb	D		D		Bb
singing	ca	-	ly	-	pso	band		playing	ca	-	ly	-	pso		band
C	C	C	C		D	E		F	F	F	F		C		F
singing	ca	-	ly	-	pso	band		playing	ca	-	ly	-	pso		band

    Video **Audio 35** **Audio 36**

Learning objectives

★ To learn • to play a new strumming pattern, the calypso strum • to sing a song and play the calypso strum at the same time.

Extras

Play **Everybody Loves Saturday Night** with these chords and strum. The calypso strum works in other styles of music like samba and even some rock songs.

Three chord tricks

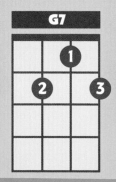

G7

SWING SHUFFLE

G7

Got myself   a tick - et gon - na...

SING AND SWING SHUFFLE

G7

Got myself a ticket, gonna take a ride
Through the Rocky Mountains to the other side,
On the train from Winnipeg and Saskatoon,
Pulling in to Jasper, we'll be leaving soon.

chorus

All aboard! We've gotta get her moving
All aboard! And she's right on time,
All aboard! We're going to Vancouver,
Shuffling along the Rocky Mountain Line.

FINGERTIPS

● Swing shuffle strum is played with a jazzy 'doo-be-doo-be-doo-be-doo' rhythm.

● Use exactly the same down-up-down-up movements as for straight shuffle strum. Play G7 and strum the rhythm 'Got myself a ticket gonna' over and over again as you sing the song.

● Play the verse melody on xylophone and make up some rhythms on percussion to accompany it.

XYLOPHONE VERSE

G		G	D		D	G		G	D		D	F		E		D
G		G	D		D	G		G	D		D	Bb		A		G (x2)

Got   myself   a tick - et, gon - na take a   ride...

G7

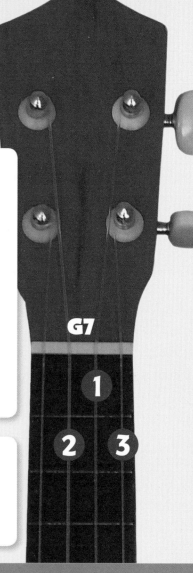

Video   **Audio 37**    **Audio 38**

Learning objectives

★ To learn ● to play G7 ● swing shuffle strum ● to arrange an instrumental verse played on xylophone, percussion and ukuleles.

Extras

Use train rhythms like 'clickety-clack' 'whooo whooo' to inspire percussion parts. ● Listen to **The Little Train of the Caipira**; **Freight Train**.

Three chord tricks

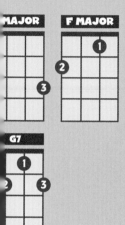

BLUES CHORD SEQUENCE

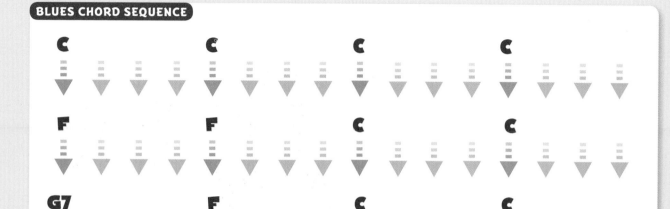

```
C          C          C          C
F          F          C          C
G7         F          C          C
```

FINGERTIPS

- Count the chord symbols in the chord sequence box. A 'twelve bar blues' is divided into twelve bars, each lasting four beats.

- Until the chord changes are familiar just strum once on each chord symbol ~ the song words remind you when to change.

- When you become more confident, you can fill in the gaps by strumming on the pulse (beat) or add a repeated rhythm like a shuffle strum.

- Notice in the song that the chord symbol is only given when the chord changes.

SING AND STRUM

C

C, play a C chord then repeat it with me,

F   C

F is the new chord then return it to C,

G7   F

Gee, it's amazing, no effort to do,

C

C what I'm saying: we're playing the blues.

   Video Audio 39 Audio 40

Learning objectives
★ To learn the 12-bar blues sequence in the key of C, using three chords.

Extras
This is the usual pattern for most blues songs and many, eg **Hard Times Blues**, can be sung over this sequence of chords.

FINGERTIPS

● Jazz and rock musicians often improvise together on the blues. Here are the notes you need to play a five-note (pentatonic) blues scale in C on the xylophone. Take all the other bars off the instrument and improvise some tunes.

● Play the blues scale on your ukulele and start improvising.

● Experiment with just using two or three of the notes to make interesting patterns (you do not have to use them all). No need to rush either ~ you can play a lazy blues as well as a busy blues.

TUNED PERCUSSION

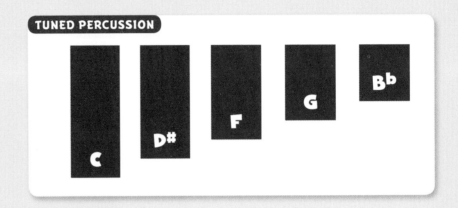

C   D#   F   G   Bb

UKULELE TAB

 Video   Audio 39 Audio 40

Learning objectives

★ To learn about the blues scale ● to use it to improvise some solos.

Extras

The blues developed from African work songs in the cotton fields of North America into songs in which a 'blue man' sang about his troubles. In the cities the blues strongly influenced the birth of jazz and rock 'n' roll.

Three chord tricks

A minor | F MAJOR

C MAJOR

FINGERTIPS

The chord symbols show when the chord changes. First strum once on each chord to begin with, then twice when the changing is easier. It's nearly always:

Am C F Am

Listen out for the two lines which are different:

Am F C

STRUM

Am		C		F		Am	

How **sad**-ly   did those **little**   pigs de - **cide** they had   to **go...**

SING AND STRUM

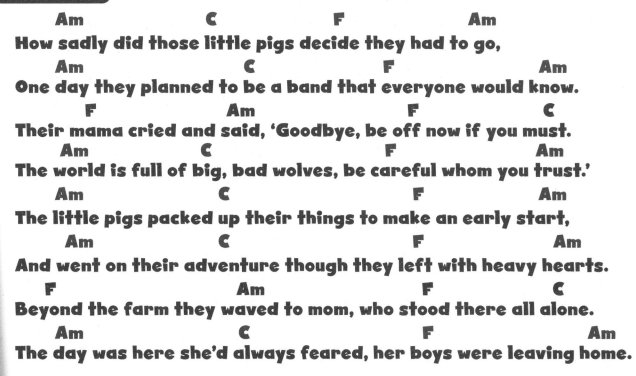

Am   C   F   Am
How sadly did those little pigs decide they had to go,

Am   C   F   Am
One day they planned to be a band that everyone would know.

         F   Am   F   C
Their mama cried and said, 'Goodbye, be off now if you must.

     Am   C   F   Am
The world is full of big, bad wolves, be careful whom you trust.'

     Am   C   F   Am
The little pigs packed up their things to make an early start,

     Am   C   F   Am
And went on their adventure though they left with heavy hearts.

     F   Am   F   C
Beyond the farm they waved to mom, who stood there all alone.

     Am   C   F   Am
The day was here she'd always feared, her boys were leaving home.

Video   Audio 41   Audio 42

Learning objectives

★ To learn • to play a three chord sequence • to play a change in chord sequence.

Extras

This song, from the musical **The Three Little Rock 'n' Roll Pigs**, is about the moment they set off to make their careers in the music industry. Can you find another musical based on a traditional story?

In South Africa

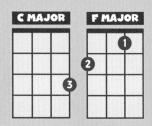

C MAJOR   F MAJOR

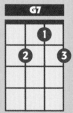

G7

STRUM

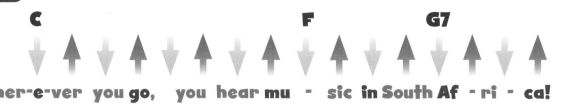

C   F   G7

Wher-e-ver you go,   you hear mu - sic in South Af - ri - ca!

SING AND STRUM

Wherever you go you hear music in South Africa!
Wherever you go you hear music in South Africa!
People singing, people dancing, people playing in the street.
From Johannesburg to Cape Town you can feel that kwela beat.
Wherever you go you hear music in South Africa!
Sa'bona! 'Hello' in Zulu. Unjani! is 'how do you do?'
Halala! is 'welcome to you!' Khalisa umcolo! Play some music!
(INSTRUMENTAL)
People singing, people dancing, people playing in the street.
From Johannesburg to Cape Town you can feel that kwela beat.
Wherever you go, you hear music in South Africa!
In Durban! In Soweto! In Free State! In Gugulethu!
Wherever you go you hear music in South Africa!
In South Africa! In South Africa! In South Africa!

FINGERTIPS

● Repeat the C (C) F G7 chord sequence throughout the song. It never changes.

● To start with, just play down strokes on the beat. When you feel confident, add a strong up stroke on the off-beats

Video   Audio 43   Audio 44

Learning objectives

★ To learn a repeating (turnaround) chord sequence
● to perform it with a song in South African kwela style.

Extras

This song is written in the style of kwela music which bega in the townships of South Africa back in the 1950's. Check out these other songs with turnaround chord sequences: **Hometown glory** by Adele and **Price tag** by Jessie J.

Three chord
tricks

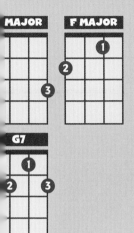

MAJOR   F MAJOR

G7

INGERTIPS

When adding new
struments to an arrangement it
important to listen carefully to
e 'balance'.

You can reduce the sound of
e more powerful instruments
playing them quietly or
mply using fewer of them.

A band should always
upport the singers, not
verpower them.

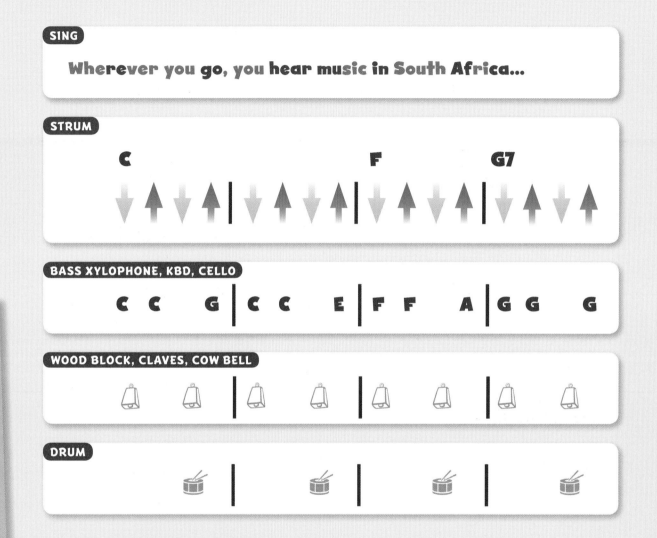

SING

Wherever you go, you hear music in South Africa...

STRUM

C   F   G7

BASS XYLOPHONE, KBD, CELLO

C C G | C C E | F F A | G G G

WOOD BLOCK, CLAVES, COW BELL

DRUM

Video

Audio 43

Audio 44

Learning objectives

★ Developing a classroom
arrangement considering •
the style of the music •
the balance required.

Extras

Check out some kwela music and you may hear other
rhythm patterns that would fit the song. Try devising
your own introduction by introducing the instruments
one at a time and building the accompaniment.

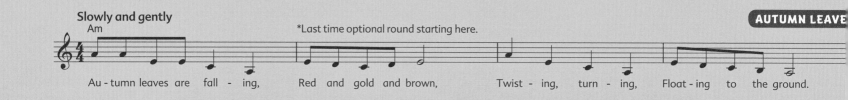

AUTUMN LEAVE[S]

Slowly and gently

Am

*Last time optional round starting here.

Au - tumn leaves are fall - ing, Red and gold and brown, Twist - ing, turn - ing, Float - ing to the ground.

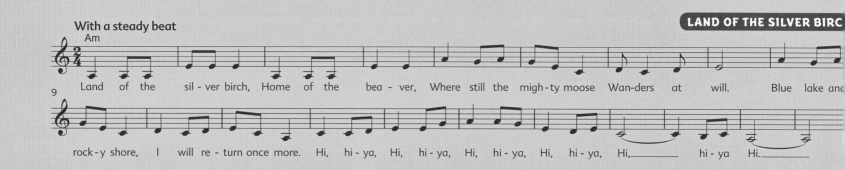

LAND OF THE SILVER BIRC[H]

With a steady beat

Am

Land of the sil - ver birch, Home of the bea - ver, Where still the migh - ty moose Wan - ders at will. Blue lake and

rock - y shore, I will re - turn once more. Hi, hi - ya, Hi, hi - ya, Hi, hi - ya, Hi, hi - ya, Hi,_____ hi - ya Hi.

F MAJOR MARC[H]

March style

F /   Last time to Coda   F /   F /

We're play-ing F   Oh yes! We're play-ing F   Oh yes!   Fin - ger num-ber 1 and fin - ger num-ber 2.
First fret on the E string, se-cond on the G,

Coda   F /

Us - ing them to-ge - ther,   see what you can do. We're play-ing Left, right, left, right, left, right, left. We're play-ing F!
Us - ing them to-ge - ther,   strum a - long with me. We're play-ing

BABOUSHK[A]

Am   F   Am   Am   F   Am   Am   F   Am   Am   F

1. Rid - ing through the   win - ter snow, Rid - ing through the   win - ter snow, Sleigh bells jin - gl - ing   as she goes. Sleigh bells jin - gl - ing
2. Christ - mas Eve Ba - boush-ka comes Christ-mas Eve Ba - boush-ka comes With a   pre-sent for   ev - 'ry - one. With a   pre-sent for

Am   Am   F   Am   Am   F   Am   Am   F   Am   Am   F   Am

as she goes.   All   o - ver Rus - sia,   all   o - ver Rus - sia, they   lis - ten for the sleigh,   they   lis - ten for the sleigh.
ev - 'ry - one.   Christ-mas is   com - ing,   Christ-mas is   com-ing, Ba - boush-ka's on her way,   Ba - boush-ka's on her way.

Relaxed calypso style

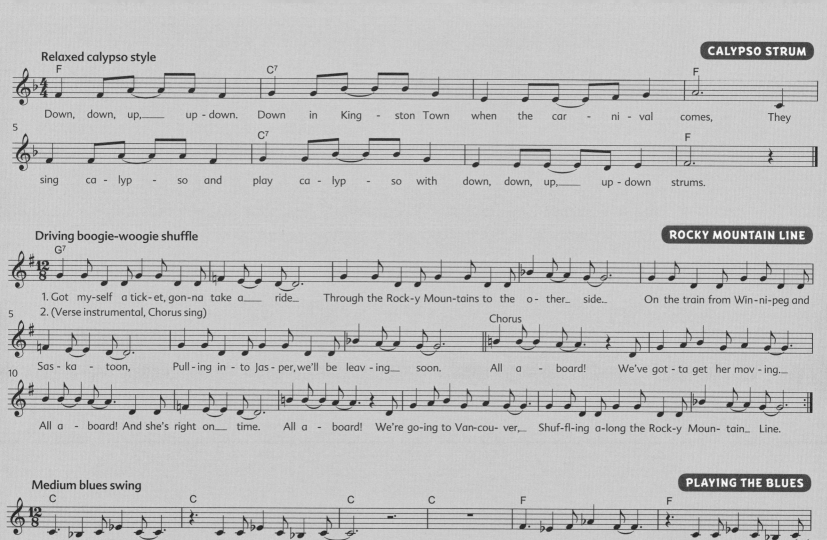

Down, down, up,___ up - down. Down in King - ston Town when the car - ni - val comes, They

sing ca - lyp - so and play ca - lyp - so with down, down, up,___ up - down strums.

Driving boogie-woogie shuffle

1. Got my-self a tick - et, gon-na take a___ ride___ Through the Rock-y Moun-tains to the o - ther_ side._ On the train from Win-ni-peg and

2. (Verse instrumental, Chorus sing)

Sas - ka - toon, Pull-ing in - to Jas-per, we'll be leav-ing_ soon. All a - board! We've got - ta get her mov-ing._

All a - board! And she's right on___ time. All a - board! We're go-ing to Van-cou-ver,___ Shuf-fl-ing a-long the Rock-y Moun- tain_ Line.

Medium blues swing

C, play a C chord then re-peat it with me.___ F is the new chord then re-turn it to C.___

— G, it's a-maz-ing,_ No F-fort to do._ C what I'm say - ing,_ we're play-ing the blues.

How sad - ly did those lit - tle pigs de - cide they had to go,___ One day they planned to

lit - tle pigs packed up their things to make an ear - ly start,___ And went on their ad -

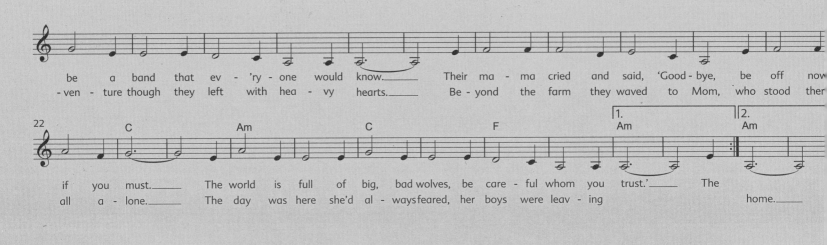

be a band that ev - 'ry - one would know.____ Their ma - ma cried and said, 'Good - bye, be off now
-ven - ture though they left with hea - vy hearts.____ Be - yond the farm they waved to Mom, who stood ther

if you must.____ The world is full of big, bad wolves, be care - ful whom you trust.'____ The
all a - lone.____ The day was here she'd al - waysfeared, her boys were leav - ing

home.____

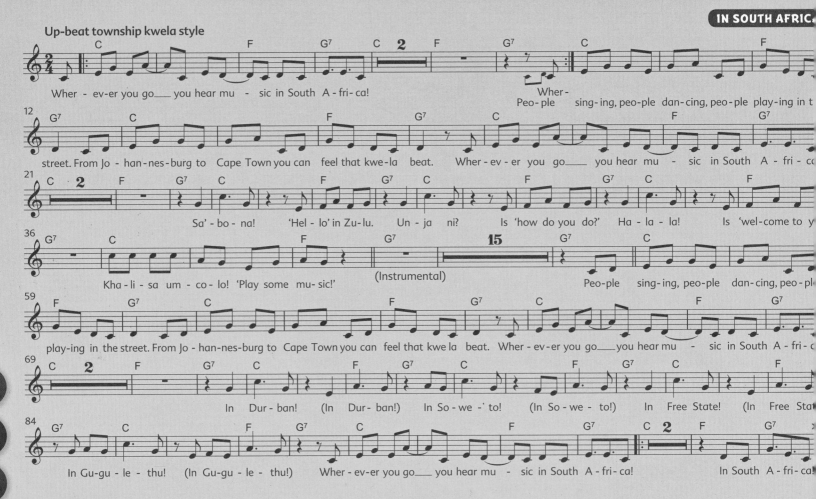

Up-beat township kwela style

Wher - ev-er you go____ you hear mu - sic in South A - fri-ca!

Wher-
Peo- ple sing-ing, peo-ple dan-cing, peo-ple play-ing in t

street. From Jo - han-nes-burg to Cape Town you can feel that kwe-la beat. Wher - ev - er you go____ you hear mu - sic in South A - fri - c

Sa' - bo - na! 'Hel - lo' in Zu - lu. Un - ja ni? Is 'how do you do?' Ha - la - la! Is 'wel-come to y

Kha - li - sa um - co - lo! 'Play some mu - sic!' (Instrumental) Peo - ple sing-ing, peo-ple dan-cing, peo-ple

play-ing in the street. From Jo - han-nes-burg to Cape Town you can feel that kwe la beat. Wher - ev-er you go____you hear mu - sic in South A - fri-c

In Dur - ban! (In Dur - ban!) In So - we -'to! (In So - we - to!) In Free State! (In Free Stat

In Gu-gu - le - thu! (In Gu-gu - le - thu!) Wher - ev-er you go____ you hear mu - sic in South A - fri-ca! In South A - fri-ca!